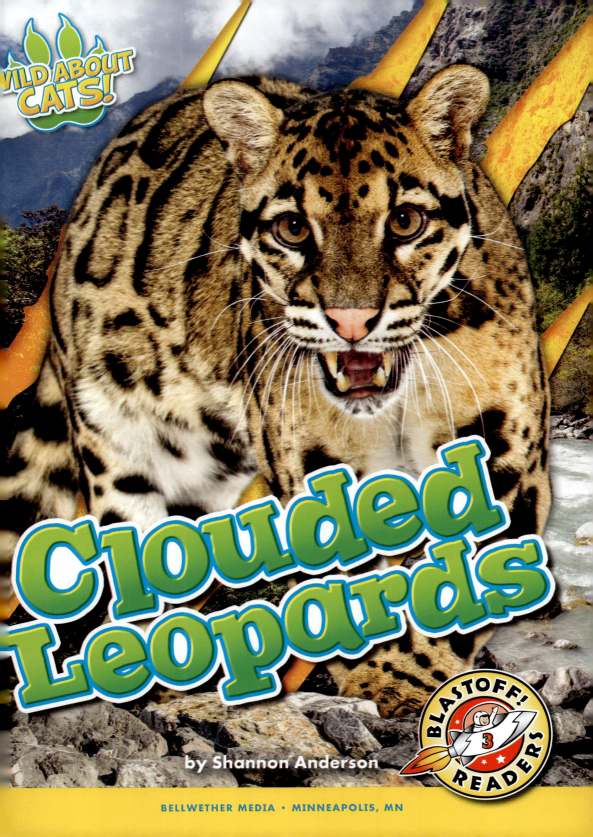

Blastoff! Readers are carefully developed by literacy experts to build reading stamina and move students toward fluency by combining standards-based content with developmentally appropriate text.

LEVELS

Level 1 provides the most support through repetition of high-frequency words, light text, predictable sentence patterns, and strong visual support.

Level 2 offers early readers a bit more challenge through varied sentences, increased text load, and text-supportive special features.

Level 3 advances early-fluent readers toward fluency through increased text load, less reliance on photos, advancing concepts, longer sentences, and more complex special features.

★ **Blastoff! Universe**

Reading Level

Grade K

Grades 1–3

Grade 4

This edition first published in 2025 by Bellwether Media, Inc.

No part of this publication may be reproduced in whole or in part without written permission of the publisher. For information regarding permission, write to Bellwether Media, Inc., Attention: Permissions Department, 6012 Blue Circle Drive, Minnetonka, MN 55343.

Library of Congress Cataloging-in-Publication Data

LC record for Clouded Leopards available at: https://lccn.loc.gov/2024046802

Text copyright © 2025 by Bellwether Media, Inc. BLASTOFF! READERS and associated logos are trademarks and/or registered trademarks of Bellwether Media, Inc.

Editor: Suzane Nguyen   Designer: Brittany McIntosh

Printed in the United States of America, North Mankato, MN.

Table of Contents

Skilled Climbers	4
Clouded Spots	8
Hidden Cats	12
Leopard Litters	18
Glossary	22
To Learn More	23
Index	24

Skilled Climbers

Clouded leopards are excellent climbers. Their ankles can turn backwards. The cats can climb down trees headfirst and hang from their back feet!

Clouded leopards live and hunt in **tropical forests** and **shrublands**.

Clouded leopards have a small range. They live in parts of southern and southeastern Asia.

Clouded Leopard Range

range = ▇

Clouded leopards are low in number. This is due to hunting and **habitat** loss.

Clouded Spots

Clouded leopards are built for climbing. They have short legs. Their large paws hold branches. Their long tails help them balance.

Cloud-shaped spots help the cats **camouflage** into the forest.

Identify a Clouded Leopard

- cloud-shaped spots
- long tail
- short legs

Clouded leopards can be over 3 feet (0.9 meters) long. Their tails are also about 3 feet (0.9 meters) long!

Size Comparison

house cat	clouded leopard
height at shoulder	**height at shoulder**
around 10 inches (25 centimeters)	around 16 inches (41 centimeters)
length (without tail)	**length (without tail)**
18 inches (46 centimeters)	around 36 inches (91 centimeters)

Males weigh up to 55 pounds (25 kilograms). Females weigh up to 30 pounds (14 kilograms).

Hidden Cats

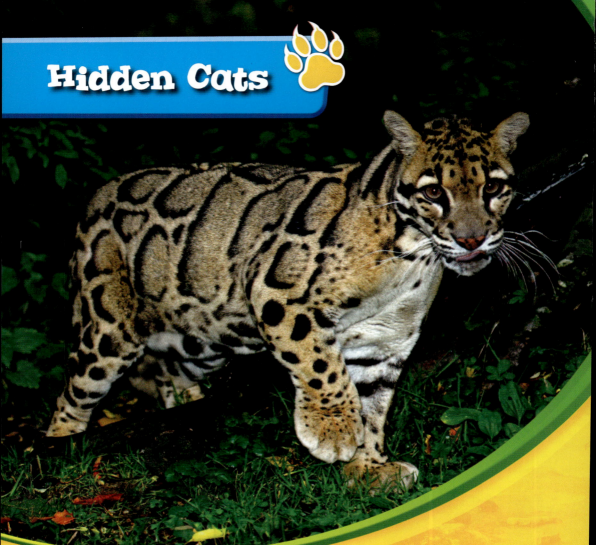

People do not see clouded leopards often. The cats are **solitary**. They are most active at night.

The cats **communicate** with each other using meows and hisses. They also growl and spit.

Clouded leopards mostly hunt on the ground. The cats have sharp claws and great eyesight.

The cats quietly sneak up on **prey**. Then they **pounce**! Sometimes they **ambush** prey from trees.

Clouded leopards are **carnivores**. Their favorite foods include wild boars and monkeys.

The cats can open their jaws wide. This allows them to take down larger prey like deer.

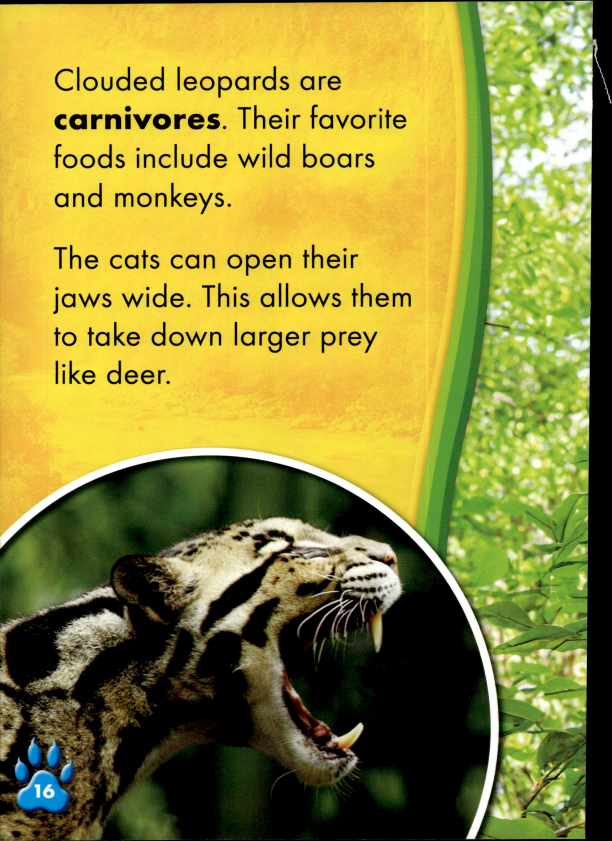

Leopard Litters

cub

Clouded leopard **litters** usually have one to five cubs. Cubs' eyes are closed for the first two weeks.

Their teeth come in after three weeks. They are big!

Baby Clouded Leopards

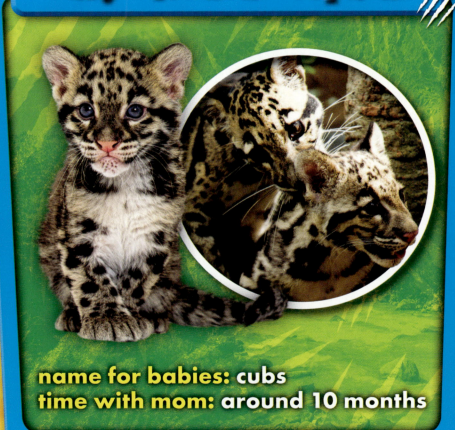

name for babies: cubs
time with mom: around 10 months

Clouded leopard cubs stop **nursing** after around three months. Then they learn to hunt from mom.

The cubs stay with their mom until they are around ten months old. Then off they go!

In the Wild

habitats:

tropical forests   shrublands

conservation status: vulnerable

| Least Concern | Near Threatened | Vulnerable | Endangered | Critically Endangered | Extinct in the Wild | Extinct |

population in the wild: fewer than 10,000
population trend: going down
life span: up to 13 years

21

Glossary

ambush—to attack from a hiding place

camouflage—to use color in order to blend in with surroundings

carnivores—animals that only eat meat

communicate—to share information and feelings

habitat—a land area with certain types of plants, animals, and weather

litters—groups of babies that are born together

nursing—drinking mom's milk

pounce—to suddenly jump onto something

prey—animals that are hunted by other animals for food

shrublands—dry lands that have mostly low plants and few trees

solitary—living alone

tropical forests—forests that grow in places that are hot and humid year-round

To Learn More

AT THE LIBRARY

Anderson, Shannon. *Snow Leopards*. Minneapolis, Minn.: Bellwether Media, 2025.

Klepeis, Alicia Z. *Leopards*. Minneapolis, Minn.: Bellwether Media, 2024.

MacDonald, Lisa. *Raising Clouded Leopards*. Huntington Beach, Calif.: Teacher Created Materials, 2019.

ON THE WEB

FACTSURFER

Factsurfer.com gives you a safe, fun way to find more information.

1. Go to www.factsurfer.com.

2. Enter "clouded leopards" into the search box and click 🔍.

3. Select your book cover to see a list of related content.

Index

ambush, 15
ankles, 4
Asia, 6
carnivores, 16
claws, 14
climb, 4, 8
communicate, 13
cubs, 18, 19, 20
eyesight, 14
feet, 4
females, 11, 20
foods, 16, 17
growl, 13
habitat loss, 7
hisses, 13
hunt, 5, 7, 14, 20
identify, 9
in the wild, 21
jaws, 16
legs, 8
litters, 18
males, 11
meows, 13
night, 12

number, 7
nursing, 20
paws, 8
pounce, 15
prey, 15, 16, 17
range, 6, 7
shrublands, 5
size, 10, 11
size comparison, 11
solitary, 12
spit, 13
spots, 9
tails, 8, 10
teeth, 19
trees, 4, 15
tropical forests, 5, 9

The images in this book are reproduced through the courtesy of: Eric Isselee, front cover (clouded leopard), pp. 3, 9, 11 (clouded leopard), 19 (left), 22; Boyloso, front cover (background); Bill Attwell/ Alamy, p. 4; Arterra Picture Library/ Alamy, p. 5; Sarah Cheriton-Jones, p. 6; slowmotiongli, pp. 8, 9 (inset); Kris Wiktor/ Alamy, pp. 10-11; Nynke van Holten, p. 11 (house cat); Gerard Lacz Images/ SuperStock, p. 12; Sandesh Kadur/ Nature Picture Library, pp. 13, 16-17; Dubrox, p. 14; glen gaffney, p. 15; AfriPics.com/ Alamy, p. 16; Piotr Krzeslak, p. 17 (wild boars); Sumruay Rattanataipob, p. 17 (stump-tailed macaques); jindrich_pavelka, p. 17 (Indian hog deer); Rufous52, pp. 18, 19 (right); Felineus, p. 20; Brian Jannsen/ Alamy, pp. 20-21.